# UNDERSTANDING ATTENTION DEFICIT HYPERACTIVE DISORDER

## Comprehensive Guide To Diagnosis, Management, And Treatment Strategies For Children And Adults

# DR. LINCOLN WAYLON

# DISCLAIMER

This book contains information that should only be used for educational and informational reasons; it is not meant to be used as a source of medical or psychological advice. The author's studies, life experiences, and expertise in the area of health and wellness served as the foundation for the content. It should not, however, be used in place of expert counsel, a diagnosis, or medical care.

Any queries you may have about a physical or mental health issue should always be directed toward the advice of a licensed healthcare provider or mental health specialist. With regard to the efficacy or outcomes of the methods or suggestions included in this book, the author and publisher make no representations or warranties.

Any information or methods in this book are used entirely at the reader's own risk and discretion. The material provided here may be used or misused, and neither the author nor the publisher will be held responsible for any results, losses, or negative impacts.

Keep in mind that everyone has different demands and reactions to health and wellness routines. Any health and wellness plans you implement must be customized to your particular circumstances, and you should speak with experts to make sure the plans meet your needs.

# TABLE OF CONTENTS

# ABOUT THE BOOK

Understanding Attention Deficit Hyperactive Disorder (ADHD) is crucial for comprehending its complexities and implications on individuals and society. This book provides a comprehensive overview of ADHD, detailing its various forms, including Inattentive, Hyperactive-Impulsive, and Combined types. By exploring common symptoms, characteristics, and demographic prevalence, the book aims to shed light on the significance of recognizing and understanding ADHD in different contexts. The importance of grasping ADHD's nuances extends beyond mere academic knowledge; it impacts effective management, support, and advocacy efforts.

The historical context of ADHD offers valuable insights into how diagnostic criteria and treatment approaches have evolved. The book delves into the history of ADHD diagnosis, highlighting key milestones in research and the influence of historical perspectives on current understanding.

Examining the evolution of treatment methodologies and current trends in ADHD comprehension provides readers with a broad perspective on how perceptions and interventions have shifted, reflecting broader changes in medical science and societal attitudes.

A deep dive into the neurological basis of ADHD reveals the critical brain structures and neurotransmitters involved in the disorder. By elucidating the genetic factors and how brain function influences behavior, the book provides a scientific foundation for understanding ADHD. This exploration of brain mechanisms helps to connect physiological processes with the behavioral symptoms observed in individuals with ADHD, offering a clearer picture of the disorder's underlying causes.

The book also covers diagnostic criteria, detailing both common and less common symptoms of ADHD. It emphasizes the importance of differentiating ADHD from other disorders and examines age-related variations in symptoms.

Understanding the various assessment tools and methods available for diagnosis is crucial for accurate identification and effective management of the disorder.

Treatment approaches and management strategies are thoroughly reviewed, including behavioral therapies, medication options, and the role of lifestyle changes. The book also explores integrative and alternative therapies, providing a well-rounded perspective on managing ADHD. Lifestyle adjustments, such as establishing routines, dietary considerations, and stress management techniques, are discussed in depth, offering practical advice for improving the quality of life for individuals with ADHD.

Support systems and resources play a pivotal role in managing ADHD. The book highlights the importance of building a robust support network, accessing community resources, and advocating for ADHD awareness. It emphasizes the role of family and caregiver support, online tools, and support groups in fostering a supportive environment for individuals with ADHD.

Addressing challenges and solutions in ADHD management, the book discusses common obstacles, practical coping strategies, and the importance of flexibility in treatment plans. It guides navigating conflicts, seeking second opinions, and adjusting approaches to treatment as needed.

Finally, the book looks ahead to future directions in ADHD research, exploring emerging trends, advances in diagnostic tools, and new treatment modalities. It considers the role of genetics and personalized medicine, as well as the impact of societal changes on ADHD understanding. Common concerns and FAQs are addressed, clarifying distinctions between ADHD and ADD, discussing diagnosis, medication side effects, and management without medication, and offering guidance for parents supporting children with ADHD.

# CHAPTER ONE

## OVERVIEW OF ATTENTION DEFICIT HYPERACTIVE DISORDER

### OVERVIEW OF ADHD

Attention Deficit Hyperactivity Disorder (ADHD) is a neurodevelopmental condition characterized by persistent patterns of inattention, hyperactivity, and impulsivity that interfere with daily functioning. ADHD can affect various aspects of life, including academic performance, occupational success, and social relationships. The disorder often manifests in childhood but can continue into adulthood, affecting individuals' ability to focus, organize tasks, and regulate behavior.

The exact causes of ADHD are not fully understood but are believed to involve a combination of genetic, environmental, and neurological factors. Studies suggest that imbalances in neurotransmitters, such as dopamine, and differences in brain structure and function contribute to the symptoms of ADHD.

Diagnosis typically involves a comprehensive evaluation by a healthcare professional, including behavioral assessments and input from multiple sources, such as parents and teachers.

Effective management of ADHD often includes a combination of behavioral strategies, educational interventions, and, in some cases, medication. Understanding ADHD is crucial for developing appropriate strategies to support individuals with the condition, both at home and in educational or workplace settings.

## COMMON SYMPTOMS AND CHARACTERISTICS

Individuals with ADHD may exhibit a range of symptoms, which are generally categorized into two main domains: inattention and hyperactivity-impulsivity. Inattention symptoms include difficulty sustaining attention, following through on tasks, and organizing activities. People with ADHD may also be prone to frequent mistakes due to careless errors and may struggle to remember details or deadlines.

Hyperactivity-impulsivity symptoms manifest as excessive fidgeting, difficulty staying seated, and a tendency to act without considering consequences. Impulsive behaviors can include interrupting others, speaking out of turn, and making hasty decisions. These symptoms can lead to challenges in both social interactions and academic or professional environments.

Recognizing these symptoms is essential for identifying ADHD and differentiating it from other conditions with similar presentations.

## TYPES OF ADHD (INATTENTIVE, HYPERACTIVE-IMPULSIVE, COMBINED)

ADHD is classified into three primary types based on the predominant symptomatology: Inattentive Type, Hyperactive-Impulsive Type, and Combined Type. The Inattentive Type is characterized mainly by symptoms of inattention, such as difficulty focusing on tasks, disorganization, and forgetfulness. This type can be particularly challenging because it may not be as visibly disruptive as hyperactivity, making it less noticeable.

The Hyperactive-Impulsive Type involves symptoms of hyperactivity and impulsivity without significant inattention. Individuals with this type may exhibit excessive movement, an inability to stay still, and impulsive actions, such as interrupting conversations or making spontaneous decisions. This type is often more apparent in social and academic settings.

The Combined Type includes a mix of both inattentive and hyperactive-impulsive symptoms. This type presents the broadest range of difficulties and may require a multifaceted approach to treatment.

## PREVALENCE AND DEMOGRAPHICS

ADHD is one of the most common neurodevelopmental disorders in children, with estimates suggesting that it affects approximately 5-7% of the global population.

The prevalence of ADHD can vary based on factors such as geographical location, cultural differences, and diagnostic practices. Research indicates that ADHD is more commonly diagnosed in boys than girls, though recent studies suggest that the gender gap may be narrowing as diagnostic criteria become more inclusive.

The disorder often persists into adulthood, with about 60% of children with ADHD continuing to experience symptoms in their adult years. ADHD can affect individuals across various socio-economic and cultural backgrounds, but the presentation and management of the disorder may be influenced by contextual factors such as access to healthcare and educational support.

Understanding the prevalence and demographics of ADHD helps in addressing public health concerns and developing targeted interventions. It also underscores the importance of early diagnosis and ongoing support for individuals with ADHD throughout their lifespan.

# IMPORTANCE OF UNDERSTANDING ADHD

Understanding ADHD is crucial for providing effective support and intervention for those affected by the disorder. Knowledge about ADHD helps educators, parents, and healthcare providers to identify symptoms early and implement appropriate strategies to manage the condition. This understanding also aids in reducing stigma and fostering a supportive environment for individuals with ADHD.

Awareness of ADHD's impact on daily functioning allows for the development of tailored educational plans and workplace accommodations that can enhance the quality of life for those affected. It also supports research and advocacy efforts aimed at improving treatment options and support services.

A thorough understanding of ADHD is essential for creating effective management strategies and fostering an inclusive environment that supports individuals with the disorder.

# CHAPTER TWO

## HISTORICAL CONTEXT

### HISTORY OF ADHD DIAGNOSIS

Attention Deficit Hyperactivity Disorder (ADHD) has a long and complex history of diagnosis, beginning in the early 20th century when it was first recognized as a distinct condition. Initially, ADHD was referred to as "Attention Deficit Disorder" and was primarily characterized by impulsivity and hyperactivity. The term "hyperkinetic impulse disorder" was used in the 1950s and 1960s, reflecting the focus on motor activity and impulsive behaviors. In 1980, the American Psychiatric Association (APA) officially included ADHD in the Diagnostic and Statistical Manual of Mental Disorders (DSM-III), providing a more standardized diagnostic framework.

The 1980s and 1990s saw a significant increase in awareness and research into ADHD, leading to the refinement of diagnostic criteria.

The DSM-IV, published in 1994, introduced more specific criteria for diagnosing ADHD, including detailed descriptions of symptoms and their impact on daily functioning. The condition was classified into three types: predominantly inattentive, predominantly hyperactive-impulsive, and combined presentation. This period marked a shift from viewing ADHD as a behavioral disorder to recognizing it as a neurodevelopmental condition.

In the 21st century, diagnostic practices have continued to evolve, with a greater emphasis on understanding ADHD as a lifelong condition that can affect various aspects of an individual's life. Recent revisions in the DSM-5, released in 2013, have refined the criteria further and extended the age of onset to 12 years old. This change acknowledges that ADHD symptoms can persist into adolescence and adulthood, providing a more comprehensive view of the disorder across the lifespan.

The treatment approaches for ADHD have undergone significant changes over the decades. Initially, treatments focused primarily on behavioral interventions, including structured routines and behavior modification techniques. Medication was a later addition, with the first stimulant medication, methylphenidate, being introduced in the 1960s. These early treatments aimed to reduce hyperactivity and improve attention by directly targeting the neurological pathways associated with the disorder.

By the 1990s, the development of additional medications and a better understanding of ADHD's neurobiological underpinnings led to more personalized treatment approaches. Non-stimulant medications, such as atomoxetine and guanfacine, were introduced, offering alternative options for individuals who did not respond well to stimulants or experienced side effects. Alongside medication, cognitive-behavioral therapy (CBT) emerged as a crucial component of treatment, helping individuals develop coping strategies and improve executive functioning skills.

In recent years, treatment approaches have become increasingly holistic, integrating medication with behavioral therapies, psychoeducation, and lifestyle modifications. Emphasis has also been placed on individualized treatment plans, recognizing that ADHD manifests differently in each person. This comprehensive approach aims to address not only the core symptoms of ADHD but also associated challenges such as academic performance, social skills, and emotional regulation.

## KEY MILESTONES IN ADHD RESEARCH

Research on ADHD has reached several key milestones that have significantly advanced our understanding of the disorder. In the 1970s, pioneering studies by researchers such as Dr. Benjamin B. Brown and Dr. Paul Wender established the validity of ADHD as a distinct clinical entity.

These studies laid the groundwork for future research and helped to differentiate ADHD from other psychiatric and behavioral disorders.

The 1990s marked another critical milestone with the advent of neuroimaging studies, which provided insights into the brain structure and function of individuals with ADHD. Functional MRI (fMRI) and PET scans revealed differences in brain activity and connectivity, particularly in areas associated with attention, impulse control, and executive functioning. These findings supported the hypothesis that ADHD has a neurobiological basis and not merely a behavioral or environmental origin.

More recently, research has focused on the genetic and environmental factors contributing to ADHD. Large-scale genetic studies have identified specific genes associated with the disorder, while longitudinal studies have examined how early life experiences and environmental influences interact with genetic predispositions. This ongoing research aims to uncover the complex interplay of factors that contribute to ADHD, paving the way for more effective and personalized interventions.

## INFLUENCE OF HISTORICAL PERSPECTIVES

Historical perspectives on ADHD have profoundly shaped the current understanding and treatment of the disorder. Early views often focused on moral or educational deficiencies, with individuals exhibiting ADHD symptoms being labeled as "troublesome" or "lazy." This stigma affected the perception of ADHD and influenced the types of interventions considered appropriate, often neglecting the underlying neurodevelopmental aspects of the disorder.

The shift towards a more scientific understanding of ADHD began in the mid-20th century, with the development of behavioral and medical frameworks for diagnosis and treatment. This change was driven by advancements in psychological research and the introduction of pharmacological treatments. As a result, ADHD began to be recognized as a legitimate neurodevelopmental disorder rather than a product of poor parenting or lack of discipline.

Today, historical perspectives continue to impact the way ADHD is perceived and treated. Increased awareness and education have helped reduce stigma and promote a more compassionate understanding of the disorder. However, challenges remain, including addressing misconceptions and ensuring that treatment approaches remain evidence-based and inclusive of the diverse experiences of individuals with ADHD.

## CURRENT TRENDS IN ADHD UNDERSTANDING

Current trends in ADHD understanding reflect a growing emphasis on a comprehensive and nuanced view of the disorder. Research has increasingly focused on recognizing ADHD as a multifaceted condition that affects not only attention and hyperactivity but also executive functioning, emotional regulation, and social interactions. This broader perspective has led to more integrative treatment approaches that combine medication, behavioral therapy, and supportive interventions tailored to individual needs.

Another significant trend is the increased recognition of ADHD across the lifespan. While ADHD was once considered primarily a childhood disorder, recent research highlights its persistence into adolescence and adulthood. This shift has led to the development of specialized interventions for older individuals, addressing issues such as academic and occupational challenges, and promoting strategies for managing ADHD symptoms throughout life.

Technology and digital tools have also become prominent in the field of ADHD. Advances in neuroimaging, genetic research, and digital health applications are providing new insights into the disorder and offering innovative approaches for diagnosis and treatment.

# CHAPTER THREE

## THE BRAIN AND ADHD

### NEUROLOGICAL BASIS OF ADHD

ADHD, or Attention Deficit Hyperactivity Disorder, has a complex neurological basis involving various brain functions and structures. Central to ADHD is a dysfunction in the brain's executive functions, which include attention control, impulse regulation, and working memory. These areas are typically managed by the prefrontal cortex, which helps in planning, decision-making, and controlling impulses. Studies have shown that individuals with ADHD often have abnormalities in this region, which can lead to difficulties in focusing and organizing tasks.

Additionally, the brain's dopaminergic system plays a crucial role in ADHD. Dopamine is a neurotransmitter essential for reward processing, motivation, and attention. In people with ADHD, there may be reduced dopamine activity in areas of the brain responsible for these functions, contributing to the symptoms of inattention and hyperactivity. This imbalance can affect the brain's ability to regulate behavior and maintain focus over extended periods.

Research into ADHD also highlights the significance of the brain's connectivity patterns. Functional imaging studies have revealed that people with ADHD often show irregularities in the connectivity between brain regions responsible for managing attention and impulse control. These connectivity issues can impact the brain's efficiency in processing and responding to stimuli, which is a core aspect of ADHD symptoms.

## KEY BRAIN STRUCTURES INVOLVED

The prefrontal cortex, basal ganglia, and cerebellum are primary brain structures implicated in ADHD. The prefrontal cortex, located at the front of the brain, is crucial for executive functions such as attention, organization, and impulse control.

In individuals with ADHD, this area may be underactive or less developed, leading to difficulties in maintaining focus and controlling impulses.

The basal ganglia, a group of structures deep within the brain, are involved in regulating motor control and executive functions.

In ADHD, these structures may exhibit abnormalities that affect motor activity and the ability to control impulses. This can contribute to the hyperactive and impulsive behaviors commonly observed in the disorder.

The cerebellum, traditionally associated with motor control, also plays a role in cognitive processes. In ADHD, the cerebellum's involvement extends beyond motor coordination to include attention and cognitive functions.

## NEUROTRANSMITTERS AND THEIR ROLE

Neurotransmitters, particularly dopamine and norepinephrine, are crucial in understanding ADHD.

Dopamine is involved in the brain's reward and pleasure centers, influencing motivation and attention. In ADHD, there is often a deficiency or imbalance in dopamine levels, which can impair the brain's ability to regulate attention and manage impulses effectively.

Norepinephrine, another key neurotransmitter, plays a role in arousal and attention. It helps in regulating alertness and concentration. In individuals with ADHD, norepinephrine levels may be disrupted, leading to problems with sustaining attention and managing responses to stimuli.

The interplay between dopamine and norepinephrine is critical in understanding how neurotransmitter imbalances contribute to ADHD symptoms.

Research has also explored how medications for ADHD, such as stimulants, work to correct these neurotransmitter imbalances. Stimulants increase the levels of dopamine and norepinephrine in the brain, helping to improve attention and reduce impulsivity.

This therapeutic approach highlights the importance of these neurotransmitters in managing ADHD symptoms.

## GENETIC FACTORS

Genetics plays a significant role in the development of ADHD, with research indicating a hereditary component to the disorder. Family studies have shown that ADHD often runs in families, suggesting that genetic factors contribute to the risk of developing the disorder. Specific genes associated with dopamine regulation and neurotransmitter function have been identified as potential contributors to ADHD susceptibility.

Genome-wide association studies (GWAS) have identified several genetic variations linked to ADHD. These variations often involve genes that influence dopamine signaling and brain development. While no single gene is responsible for ADHD, the combined effect of multiple genetic factors can increase the likelihood of developing the disorder.

Understanding the genetic basis of ADHD can help in developing personalized approaches to treatment and management. Genetic research also aids in identifying individuals at higher risk for ADHD, potentially leading to earlier diagnosis and intervention strategies.

## HOW BRAIN FUNCTION AFFECTS BEHAVIOR

The way brain function affects behavior in ADHD is evident in the challenges individuals face with attention, impulse control, and hyperactivity. The disruptions in brain structures and neurotransmitter systems lead to difficulties in regulating attention and behavior. For instance, problems with the prefrontal cortex can result in difficulties with planning and executing tasks, while issues in the basal ganglia can affect impulse control and motor activity.

Behavioral symptoms of ADHD, such as inattention, restlessness, and impulsivity, are directly linked to these brain function disruptions. Impaired executive functions can lead to struggles with organizing tasks, following through with responsibilities, and controlling spontaneous actions. Understanding these connections helps in tailoring behavioral interventions and therapeutic strategies to address the specific challenges faced by individuals with ADHD.

Additionally, the interaction between brain function and behavior underscores the importance of targeted treatment approaches. For example, behavioral therapies and medications that address the underlying neurological issues can help improve attention and impulse control, enhancing overall functioning and quality of life for individuals with ADHD.

# CHAPTER FOUR

## ADHD SYMPTOMS AND DIAGNOSIS

### DIAGNOSTIC CRITERIA

Diagnosing Attention Deficit Hyperactivity Disorder (ADHD) involves meeting specific criteria outlined in the Diagnostic and Statistical Manual of Mental Disorders (DSM-5).

For an accurate diagnosis, individuals must display a persistent pattern of inattention and/or hyperactivity-impulsivity that interferes with functioning or development. Inattention includes difficulties sustaining focus, organizing tasks, and following through on instructions, while hyperactivity-impulsivity is characterized by excessive fidgeting, restlessness, and difficulty waiting for one's turn. These symptoms should be present for at least six months and be inappropriate for the individual's developmental level.

The DSM-5 requires that symptoms cause significant impairment in social, academic, or occupational functioning. To ensure a correct diagnosis, symptoms must be observed in at least two different settings, such as home and school or work. Additionally, the onset of symptoms should occur before the age of 12, although the disorder may not be recognized until later. Professionals often use a combination of clinical interviews, behavioral observations, and input from family and teachers to determine if the diagnostic criteria are met.

Other potential causes or conditions must be ruled out before concluding an ADHD diagnosis. For instance, symptoms must not be better explained by another mental disorder, such as mood disorders or anxiety disorders, and must not be attributable to substance abuse or medical conditions. A thorough evaluation helps to ensure an accurate diagnosis and appropriate intervention.

## COMMON AND LESS COMMON SYMPTOMS

ADHD manifests through a range of symptoms that can significantly affect daily life. Common symptoms include inattention, such as difficulty staying focused, frequent mistakes due to careless errors, and a tendency to forget or lose things. Hyperactive symptoms involve an inability to remain seated, excessive talking, and difficulty engaging in activities quietly. Impulsivity is marked by hasty decisions without considering consequences, interrupting others, and difficulty waiting for one's turn.

Less common symptoms of ADHD might include emotional dysregulation, such as sudden mood swings or difficulty managing frustration, and sensory processing issues, like an aversion to certain textures or sounds. Individuals may also exhibit atypical responses to environmental stimuli, such as becoming easily overwhelmed or distracted by external noise. Recognizing these less common symptoms is important for a comprehensive understanding of how ADHD affects various aspects of an individual's behavior and functioning.

While these symptoms can vary widely among individuals, they typically disrupt functioning in multiple settings. It's essential to observe the persistence and severity of symptoms across different environments to distinguish ADHD from other conditions and ensure a complete assessment.

## DIFFERENTIATING ADHD FROM OTHER DISORDERS

Distinguishing ADHD from other mental health conditions is vital for effective treatment. ADHD shares symptoms with several other disorders, including anxiety disorders, mood disorders, and learning disabilities. For example, individuals with anxiety may also display restlessness and difficulty concentrating, while those with mood disorders may show impulsivity and emotional instability. Careful assessment helps to differentiate ADHD by focusing on the specific patterns and contexts of symptoms.

A key strategy in differentiating ADHD from other disorders is a thorough clinical evaluation that includes detailed patient history, symptom assessment, and observational data from multiple settings.

Professionals often use standardized rating scales and diagnostic interviews to assess the presence and impact of symptoms. Additionally, understanding the temporal aspects of symptoms—such as their onset, duration, and persistence—is crucial for distinguishing ADHD from conditions with similar features.

Collateral information from family, teachers, and other significant individuals provides valuable insights into the behavior and functioning of the individual across different environments. This comprehensive approach helps in accurately diagnosing ADHD and ruling out other conditions that may present with overlapping symptoms.

# AGE-RELATED SYMPTOM VARIATIONS

ADHD symptoms can manifest differently across various age groups, influencing diagnosis and treatment approaches. In children, symptoms often include hyperactivity and impulsivity, such as excessive movement and difficulty remaining seated. As individuals age, symptoms may evolve, with adolescents and adults experiencing more internalized symptoms like disorganization, procrastination, and difficulty focusing on tasks for extended periods.

In adults, ADHD symptoms might become less overt but can still cause significant impairment. Adults may struggle with time management, organization, and maintaining relationships. They might also experience difficulties in maintaining employment and managing daily responsibilities. The shift from hyperactivity to more subtle forms of inattention and executive function challenges often necessitates a different approach to management and treatment.

Age-related variations in symptoms highlight the importance of ongoing evaluation and tailored interventions. Regular monitoring and adjustments to treatment strategies ensure that the evolving needs of individuals with ADHD are effectively addressed throughout their lifespan.

## ASSESSMENT TOOLS AND METHODS

Assessment tools and methods for diagnosing ADHD are multifaceted and designed to capture a comprehensive picture of an individual's symptoms and functioning. Common tools include standardized rating scales, such as the Conners' Rating Scale and the ADHD Rating Scale-IV, which are used to gather information from multiple sources, including parents, teachers, and the individual themselves. These tools help quantify the frequency and severity of symptoms, aiding in diagnosis and treatment planning.

Clinical interviews and behavioral observations are also integral components of the assessment process.

Structured interviews, such as the ADHD Clinical Diagnostic Interview, provide a detailed exploration of symptom history, onset, and impact on daily functioning. Observational methods involve monitoring behavior in various settings to assess the consistency and context of symptoms, which is crucial for accurate diagnosis.

Additionally, neuropsychological testing may be employed to evaluate cognitive functions such as attention, executive functioning, and working memory. This comprehensive approach ensures that all aspects of the individual's functioning are considered, leading to a more accurate diagnosis and effective treatment plan.

# CHAPTER FIVE

## TREATMENT APPROACHES AND MANAGEMENT

### OVERVIEW OF TREATMENT OPTIONS

Attention Deficit Hyperactivity Disorder (ADHD) is managed through a multifaceted approach, combining various treatment options to address its symptoms. The primary treatments include behavioral therapies, medication, lifestyle changes, and integrative approaches. Each option aims to alleviate symptoms such as inattention, hyperactivity, and impulsivity and is tailored to the individual's unique needs and challenges. Healthcare providers often recommend a combination of these treatments to achieve the best outcomes.

Behavioral therapies focus on modifying specific behaviors and improving organizational skills, social interactions, and emotional regulation. Medication, on the other hand, helps manage the neurobiological aspects of ADHD by balancing brain chemicals.

Lifestyle changes, such as structured routines and dietary adjustments, can also play a significant role in managing symptoms. Integrative therapies, like mindfulness or yoga, offer additional support by promoting overall well-being.

Understanding these treatment options enables families and individuals to make informed decisions about managing ADHD. Collaboration with healthcare professionals is essential in developing a comprehensive treatment plan that addresses both immediate symptoms and long-term needs.

## BEHAVIORAL THERAPIES

Behavioral therapies for ADHD emphasize altering negative behaviors and reinforcing positive ones. This often involves techniques such as cognitive-behavioral therapy (CBT), which helps individuals develop coping strategies and problem-solving skills. Therapists work with patients to set specific goals, track progress, and modify behaviors through rewards and consequences, which can improve self-control and reduce impulsivity.

Parents and teachers are often involved in behavioral therapies to ensure consistency in implementing strategies across different environments. This may include creating structured routines, using visual aids to remind children of tasks, and reinforcing desirable behaviors through positive reinforcement. Training in these techniques helps adults effectively support children with ADHD in managing their behaviors.

Regular assessment and adjustment of therapy plans are crucial to address changing needs and ensure that strategies remain effective. Behavioral therapies are a foundational component of ADHD management, providing tools and skills that can lead to lasting improvements in behavior and functioning.

## MEDICATION TYPES AND THEIR EFFECTS

Medication for ADHD typically includes stimulants and non-stimulants. Stimulants, such as methylphenidate and amphetamines, are the most commonly prescribed and work by increasing levels of neurotransmitters in the brain, which helps improve attention and reduce hyperactivity and impulsivity. These medications are usually effective and fast-acting but may have side effects like insomnia or appetite loss.

Non-stimulants, such as atomoxetine and guanfacine, offer alternatives for individuals who cannot tolerate stimulants or have not responded well to them. Non-stimulants work differently by affecting neurotransmitter systems and can be beneficial for managing symptoms with potentially fewer side effects. They often have a slower onset but provide a steady level of symptom control throughout the day.

Medication management involves careful monitoring by healthcare providers to adjust dosages and address any side effects. Collaboration between the patient, their family, and the prescribing doctor ensures that the chosen medication effectively addresses symptoms while minimizing adverse effects.

# ROLE OF LIFESTYLE CHANGES

Lifestyle changes play a crucial role in managing ADHD symptoms and enhancing overall well-being. Establishing consistent routines, such as regular sleep schedules and structured daily activities, can help improve organization and reduce forgetfulness. Creating a calm and organized environment can also reduce distractions and support better focus and task completion.

Dietary modifications, like incorporating a balanced diet rich in proteins and complex carbohydrates, may support brain function and help stabilize energy levels. Avoiding excessive sugar and caffeine can prevent exacerbation of hyperactive symptoms. Regular physical activity, such as exercise or sports, helps channel excess energy and improves concentration and mood.

Adopting mindfulness practices, like meditation or yoga, can enhance self-regulation and reduce stress.

# INTEGRATIVE AND ALTERNATIVE THERAPIES

Integrative and alternative therapies offer additional support for managing ADHD symptoms by focusing on holistic well-being. Approaches such as mindfulness-based practices, yoga, and acupuncture can help individuals develop greater self-awareness and improve focus and emotional regulation. These therapies address both physical and mental health aspects, providing a balanced approach to treatment.

Nutritional supplements, such as omega-3 fatty acids and zinc, are sometimes used to complement conventional treatments. Research on their effectiveness is ongoing, but some studies suggest that they may support cognitive function and reduce ADHD symptoms. It is important to consult healthcare providers before starting any supplements to ensure they are appropriate and safe.

Integrative therapies can enhance overall treatment plans by providing additional tools and strategies for managing ADHD.

# CHAPTER SIX

## BEHAVIORAL THERAPY FOR ADHD

## PRINCIPLES OF BEHAVIORAL THERAPY

Behavioral therapy for ADHD is grounded in the principle that behavior is learned and can be modified through reinforcement and systematic change. The core idea is to identify specific, observable behaviors that need to be addressed, such as impulsivity or inattention, and use rewards and consequences to encourage desirable behaviors while reducing problematic ones. This approach is often structured around setting clear, achievable goals and breaking down complex behaviors into manageable steps, making it easier for individuals with ADHD to follow through and succeed.

A fundamental aspect of behavioral therapy is the use of positive reinforcement to encourage desired behaviors. This involves providing rewards or praise when the individual demonstrates appropriate behavior, which helps to strengthen these behaviors over time. Conversely, undesirable behaviors are addressed through strategies like planned ignoring or logical consequences, which aim to decrease their frequency without fostering resentment or frustration. The therapy is tailored to each individual, focusing on personal strengths and challenges to create a personalized improvement plan.

Consistency is crucial in behavioral therapy. This means that the strategies and interventions used must be applied consistently by all involved—therapists, parents, and educators. The therapy involves regular monitoring and adjustments based on the individual's progress.

By maintaining consistency in applying behavioral techniques and reinforcement strategies, individuals with ADHD are more likely to experience sustained improvements in their behavior and functioning.

Behavioral therapy employs various techniques and strategies to address ADHD symptoms. One common technique is the use of behavior modification charts or token systems, where individuals earn tokens or points for exhibiting positive behaviors, which can later be exchanged for rewards.

This visual representation of progress helps maintain motivation and provides immediate feedback. Another effective strategy is the use of structured routines and schedules to help individuals with ADHD manage their time and responsibilities more effectively.

Cognitive-behavioral techniques are also utilized, focusing on changing thought patterns that may contribute to problematic behaviors. This involves helping individuals recognize and challenge negative or distorted thoughts that may lead to impulsive actions or difficulties with attention. Techniques such as self-monitoring, where individuals track their behavior and progress, are also commonly used to foster self-awareness and self-regulation.

Social skills training is another essential component of behavioral therapy for ADHD. This involves teaching individuals how to interact appropriately with peers, manage conflicts, and develop effective communication skills. Role-playing and practice scenarios are used to help individuals learn and apply these skills in real-life situations, promoting better social interactions and reducing instances of socially disruptive behavior.

## ROLE OF PARENTS AND CAREGIVERS

Parents and caregivers play a crucial role in the success of behavioral therapy for ADHD. They are often involved in implementing and reinforcing the strategies and techniques learned during therapy sessions. This includes using consistent discipline and reward systems at home, setting up structured routines, and providing encouragement and support to help the individual adhere to their behavior plan.

Collaboration between parents and therapists ensures that strategies are effectively applied in both therapeutic and home environments.

Training for parents and caregivers is typically a part of behavioral therapy programs. This training helps them understand the principles of behavior management and how to apply them effectively. Parents are taught how to set realistic expectations, provide appropriate reinforcement, and handle challenging behaviors constructively. This empowerment allows them to create a supportive environment that fosters positive behavioral changes.

Regular communication between parents, caregivers, and therapists is essential for tracking progress and making necessary adjustments to the behavior plan. This collaborative approach ensures that any issues or concerns are addressed promptly and that the therapy remains aligned with the individual's evolving needs. By working together, parents and therapists can maximize the effectiveness of behavioral interventions and support the individual's growth and development.

## EVALUATING THERAPY EFFECTIVENESS

Evaluating the effectiveness of behavioral therapy involves regularly assessing progress toward set goals and making data-driven decisions. Therapists use various methods, such as behavior rating scales, observation, and feedback from parents and teachers, to measure changes in behavior and academic performance. This data helps in determining whether the therapy is achieving its intended outcomes and identifies areas where additional adjustments may be needed.

Regular reviews and updates to the behavior plan are crucial for maintaining therapy effectiveness. This involves analyzing data collected from progress reports and adjusting strategies as needed to address any emerging challenges or changes in the individual's needs. Periodic evaluations ensure that the therapy remains relevant and effective, helping individuals with ADHD continue to make meaningful progress.

In addition to measuring behavioral changes, evaluating the impact on overall quality of life is important. This includes assessing improvements in social interactions, academic performance, and self-esteem. Effective therapy should not only reduce problematic behaviors but also enhance the individual's overall functioning and well-being. Comprehensive evaluation helps ensure that all aspects of the individual's life are positively affected by the therapy.

## INTEGRATING THERAPY WITH OTHER TREATMENTS

Integrating behavioral therapy with other treatments can enhance overall effectiveness for individuals with ADHD. This often involves combining behavioral strategies with medication management, educational support, and other therapeutic approaches. For instance, medication may help manage core symptoms of ADHD, such as inattention and hyperactivity, while behavioral therapy addresses specific behavioral issues and teaches coping strategies.

Collaboration between different healthcare providers, such as psychiatrists, psychologists, and educational professionals, is essential for a holistic approach. Coordinated care ensures that all aspects of the individual's treatment plan are aligned and that therapy is complementary to other interventions. This collaborative approach helps in creating a comprehensive treatment plan that addresses both the symptoms of ADHD and any related challenges.

Family involvement is also crucial in integrating therapy with other treatments. Parents and caregivers need to be informed and involved in all aspects of the treatment plan, including medication management and educational accommodations.

# CHAPTER SEVEN

## LIFESTYLE ADJUSTMENTS FOR ADHD

### IMPORTANCE OF ROUTINE AND ORGANIZATION

Establishing a consistent daily routine is crucial for managing ADHD. A structured schedule helps in creating predictability, which can reduce the chaos that often accompanies ADHD.

Begin by setting specific times for waking up, eating meals, and going to bed. Utilize tools like planners or digital apps to create a daily checklist that includes tasks and appointments. This helps in visualizing the day and staying focused on priorities.

Organizational tools such as labeled bins, drawers, and to-do lists can make a significant difference. Designate specific places for frequently used items, which minimize the time spent searching for things and reduce distractions. Developing a system for organizing your workspace or home, like color-coded folders for documents or a bulletin board for important reminders, can enhance overall efficiency and decrease the cognitive load of managing various tasks.

Incorporating these organizational strategies into your routine can lead to increased productivity and reduced stress. By consistently following a well-structured schedule and maintaining an organized environment, individuals with ADHD can better manage their time and responsibilities.

This systematic approach can also foster a sense of accomplishment and control, which is particularly beneficial for those struggling with ADHD-related challenges.

## DIETARY CONSIDERATIONS

Diet plays a significant role in managing ADHD symptoms. Focusing on a balanced diet rich in fruits, vegetables, whole grains, and lean proteins can support cognitive function and overall well-being.

Omega-3 fatty acids, found in fish like salmon and supplements, are particularly beneficial for brain health and can help with concentration and mood regulation. Reducing the intake of processed foods and sugars is also crucial, as these can exacerbate ADHD symptoms by causing fluctuations in blood sugar levels.

Meal planning and regular eating times are essential for maintaining stable energy levels throughout the day. Aim to have smaller, balanced meals and snacks at regular intervals to avoid energy crashes and mood swings.

Staying hydrated by drinking plenty of water can also support cognitive function and overall health. Consider keeping a food diary to identify any dietary patterns that may affect ADHD symptoms and make adjustments as needed.

Consulting with a healthcare professional or nutritionist can provide personalized guidance and ensure that dietary changes are beneficial and appropriate. They can help tailor dietary recommendations based on individual needs, preferences, and any other health conditions that may be present, making it easier to implement a diet that supports managing ADHD effectively.

## EXERCISE AND PHYSICAL ACTIVITY

Regular physical activity is highly beneficial for managing ADHD symptoms. Engaging in aerobic exercises, such as running, swimming, or cycling, can improve focus, reduce hyperactivity, and enhance mood.

Aim for at least 30 minutes of moderate exercise most days of the week. Incorporating activities that you enjoy can make it easier to maintain a consistent exercise routine and integrate it into your lifestyle.

Strength training and activities that require coordination, such as dancing or martial arts, can also be beneficial. These types of exercises help in improving impulse control and executive functioning.

Finding ways to incorporate physical activity into daily routines, such as taking the stairs instead of the elevator or walking during breaks, can help increase overall activity levels.

Creating a structured exercise routine and setting achievable goals can contribute to long-term success. Tracking progress, celebrating milestones, and staying motivated through fitness classes or workout groups can enhance adherence to an exercise regimen. Regular physical activity not only supports ADHD management but also promotes overall health and well-being.

## SLEEP HYGIENE AND ITS IMPACT

Good sleep hygiene is essential for managing ADHD symptoms, as quality sleep directly impacts attention, mood, and cognitive function. Establishing a consistent sleep schedule, with regular bedtimes and wake-up times, helps regulate the body's internal clock and improves sleep quality. Create a calming pre-sleep routine, such as reading or taking a warm bath, to signal to your body that it is time to wind down.

Creating an optimal sleep environment is also crucial. Ensure your bedroom is cool, dark, and quiet to facilitate better sleep.

Avoid screens and stimulating activities before bedtime, as the blue light emitted by devices can interfere with melatonin production and disrupt sleep patterns. Limiting caffeine and heavy meals in the evening can also prevent sleep disturbances.

Addressing any sleep issues with a healthcare provider is important if problems persist. They can offer guidance on sleep disorders or other factors that may be affecting your sleep quality. Prioritizing sleep hygiene can lead to improved daily functioning and better management of ADHD symptoms, enhancing overall quality of life.

# STRESS MANAGEMENT TECHNIQUES

Effective stress management is crucial for individuals with ADHD, as stress can exacerbate symptoms and impact overall functioning. Techniques such as mindfulness meditation, deep breathing exercises, and progressive muscle relaxation can help manage stress and improve focus. Setting aside time each day for relaxation and self-care practices can help reduce anxiety and enhance emotional resilience.

Establishing healthy boundaries and managing time effectively can also reduce stress. Prioritize tasks, break them into manageable steps, and use tools like planners or time management apps to stay organized. Learning to delegate or ask for help when needed can prevent overwhelm and maintain balance in daily life.

Engaging in hobbies and activities that bring joy and relaxation can provide a healthy outlet for stress. Whether it's spending time outdoors, pursuing creative interests, or connecting with friends, finding enjoyable activities can improve overall well-being and help manage ADHD symptoms. Regularly incorporating stress management techniques into daily routines can support better mental health and enhance quality of life.

# CHAPTER EIGHT

## SUPPORT SYSTEMS AND RESOURCES

### BUILDING A SUPPORT NETWORK

Establishing a robust support network is essential for managing Attention Deficit Hyperactive Disorder (ADHD). Begin by identifying key individuals who can offer support, such as family members, friends, and professionals like therapists or counselors. These people should be understanding of ADHD and willing to collaborate on strategies that work best for the individual. Engaging in open conversations about ADHD helps in setting expectations and clarifying how they can provide support, whether through encouragement, understanding, or practical help with daily tasks.

Next, consider joining local support groups where individuals with ADHD and their families can share experiences and strategies. These groups offer a sense of community and validation, providing a space to discuss challenges and successes. Engaging with others who have similar experiences can offer practical advice and emotional support, which can be invaluable for managing ADHD. It's also helpful to build relationships with professionals who specialize in ADHD to gain additional insights and guidance.

Finally, integrate the support network into daily routines to ensure that support is consistent and effective. This can include regular check-ins with supportive individuals, attending support group meetings, and maintaining communication with professionals. Building a reliable support system takes time and effort but is crucial for navigating the complexities of ADHD and enhancing overall well-being.

## SUPPORT GROUPS AND COMMUNITY RESOURCES

Support groups and community resources are vital for those managing ADHD. These groups offer a platform for sharing experiences, learning new coping strategies, and receiving emotional support from others in similar situations. Participating in these groups provides a sense of belonging and understanding, which can be particularly reassuring for individuals dealing with the challenges of ADHD. Regular attendance can also foster deeper connections and provide ongoing motivation.

Community resources such as local health organizations and educational institutions often offer programs specifically designed for individuals with ADHD.

These programs may include workshops, educational sessions, and social events that address various aspects of ADHD management. By taking advantage of these resources, individuals can access valuable information, practical tools, and community connections that support their ADHD journey.

Additionally, many communities have online platforms and directories that list support groups and resources. Utilizing these platforms can help individuals find and connect with relevant groups and services. This can be particularly useful for those who may have limited access to in-person resources or prefer the convenience of virtual support.

ONLINE TOOLS AND RESOURCES

Online tools and resources are essential for managing ADHD effectively. Numerous websites, apps, and platforms offer tailored solutions such as organizational tools, reminders, and educational content. Tools like task management apps can help individuals break down tasks into manageable steps and set reminders to stay on track. Utilizing these tools can enhance productivity and help manage daily responsibilities more efficiently.

Educational websites and forums dedicated to ADHD provide valuable information on the condition, including strategies for managing symptoms and personal stories from others with ADHD. Engaging with these resources can offer insights into effective management techniques and connect individuals with a broader community.

Online forums also provide a space to ask questions and receive advice from those who have firsthand experience with ADHD.

In addition to tools and educational resources, online therapy, and coaching services can provide support from the comfort of one's home. These services often offer personalized strategies and ongoing support, which can be particularly beneficial for individuals seeking flexible options for managing their ADHD. Exploring these online resources can greatly contribute to effective ADHD management.

## FAMILY AND CAREGIVER SUPPORT

Family and caregiver support is crucial for individuals with ADHD, as these key figures play a significant role in daily life and management. Educating family members and caregivers about ADHD is the first step in ensuring they understand the condition and its impact. This education can help them better support the individual by recognizing symptoms and responding appropriately to challenges.

Caregivers should be involved in developing and implementing management strategies, such as creating structured routines and setting up organizational systems.

Regular communication between the individual with ADHD and their caregivers helps in adjusting strategies as needed and addressing any emerging issues. Encouraging caregivers to attend support groups or seek their counseling can also be beneficial, providing them with tools and strategies to manage their role effectively.

Maintaining open lines of communication and providing emotional support are essential aspects of caregiver involvement. Recognizing and appreciating the efforts of family members and caregivers can foster a supportive environment and strengthen relationships. This collaborative approach ensures that the individual with ADHD has a reliable support system to navigate daily challenges.

Advocating for ADHD awareness involves educating the public about the condition to promote understanding and reduce stigma. This can be done through various means, such as participating in awareness campaigns, sharing personal stories, and engaging in public speaking opportunities. Raising awareness helps in creating a more informed society that recognizes ADHD as a legitimate and manageable condition.

Working with local organizations and educational institutions to host workshops and seminars can also contribute to broader awareness. These events provide opportunities for people to learn about ADHD, its symptoms, and effective management strategies. Collaboration with schools and community groups can help integrate ADHD awareness into educational programs and support systems.

Advocating for ADHD awareness includes engaging with policymakers to influence legislation and funding for ADHD research and resources. Supporting policies that promote better diagnosis, treatment options, and educational support for individuals with ADHD can have a lasting impact on improving the quality of life for those affected. By actively participating in advocacy efforts, individuals can contribute to a more supportive and informed community.

# CHAPTER NINE

## CHALLENGES AND SOLUTIONS IN ADHD MANAGEMENT

## COMMON OBSTACLES IN TREATMENT

Managing ADHD presents various challenges that can hinder effective treatment. One significant obstacle is the variability in symptoms and their impact on daily functioning. Individuals with ADHD may experience fluctuating levels of attention, impulsivity, and hyperactivity, making it difficult to find a one-size-fits-all approach. Additionally, co-occurring conditions, such as anxiety or depression, can complicate treatment by masking or exacerbating ADHD symptoms, leading to a less straightforward diagnosis and treatment process.

Another common challenge is adherence to treatment protocols. Consistency in medication and behavioral strategies is crucial for managing ADHD effectively; yet maintaining this consistency can be difficult due to forgetfulness, lifestyle changes, or a lack of immediate feedback on the effectiveness of treatment. Moreover, the stigma associated with ADHD and its treatments can affect a person's willingness to seek help or stick with a prescribed regimen.

Environmental factors, such as chaotic home life or unsupportive school or work environments, can also impede treatment progress.

These external stressors can exacerbate symptoms and hinder the implementation of coping strategies. It is essential to recognize these obstacles and address them to enhance the overall effectiveness of ADHD management strategies.

## PRACTICAL SOLUTIONS AND COPING STRATEGIES

To overcome obstacles in ADHD treatment, practical solutions and coping strategies are vital. Developing a structured routine is an effective way to manage ADHD symptoms. This includes using tools such as planners, reminders, and alarms to help maintain focus and organization.

Establishing consistent daily habits can reduce the impact of symptoms on daily life and enhance overall functioning.

Behavioral strategies, such as cognitive-behavioral therapy (CBT), can also play a significant role in managing ADHD. CBT helps individuals develop skills to manage impulsivity, improve time management, and address negative thought patterns. Implementing mindfulness and relaxation techniques can further support emotional regulation and reduce stress, contributing to a more balanced approach to managing symptoms.

Engaging in supportive communities or peer groups can provide additional benefits. These groups offer a space for individuals to share experiences, exchange practical tips, and receive encouragement. Such social support networks can enhance motivation and provide valuable insights into effective coping strategies.

Conflicts and setbacks are an inevitable part of ADHD management. When treatment plans do not yield the expected results, it is crucial to address these issues promptly. Open communication with healthcare providers is essential in these situations. Discussing concerns and changes in symptoms can lead to adjustments in treatment plans that better address the individual's needs.

Learning to manage setbacks involves recognizing that progress may be non-linear. It is important to approach setbacks with patience and resilience. Reflecting on what may have led to the setback and identifying any changes in routines, medication, or external factors can provide insights into how to overcome these challenges and get back on track.

Developing problem-solving skills and coping strategies can also help manage conflicts. For example, setting realistic goals and breaking them into smaller, manageable tasks can make challenges feel less overwhelming. Celebrating small victories and maintaining a positive outlook can assist in overcoming obstacles and maintaining motivation throughout the treatment process.

## ADJUSTING TREATMENT PLANS

Adjusting treatment plans is a critical aspect of managing ADHD effectively. Treatment plans may need modification based on changes in symptoms, life circumstances, or responses to medication. Regular follow-ups with healthcare providers are necessary to evaluate the effectiveness of current strategies and make informed decisions about adjustments.

When adjustments are required, it is essential to consider a comprehensive approach. This may involve altering medication dosages, incorporating new therapeutic techniques, or integrating additional support services. For example, if a particular medication is not producing the desired results, a different medication or combination of treatments may be explored.

Collaborating with healthcare professionals to adjust treatment plans ensures that changes are evidence-based and tailored to the individual's evolving needs. It is also important for individuals to actively participate in this process, providing feedback on their experiences and symptoms to help guide adjustments effectively.

## SEEKING SECOND OPINIONS

Seeking second opinions can be a valuable step in ADHD management, especially when treatment outcomes are unsatisfactory or when facing complex cases. Consulting with another healthcare provider can offer fresh perspectives and alternative treatment approaches. Different professionals may have varied experiences and insights, potentially leading to more effective management strategies.

When seeking a second opinion, it is helpful to gather comprehensive information about your current treatment, including medication, therapy, and any other interventions.

This will enable the new provider to make an informed assessment and provide recommendations based on a full understanding of your situation.

Second opinions can also serve to confirm or challenge existing diagnoses and treatment plans. This process not only offers reassurance but can also uncover new treatment options or adjustments that may better address individual needs. Engaging in this proactive approach helps ensure that the treatment plan is optimized for the best possible outcomes.

# CHAPTER TEN

## FUTURE DIRECTIONS IN ADHD RESEARCH

### ADVANCES IN DIAGNOSTIC TOOLS

Recent advancements in diagnostic tools have revolutionized the way Attention Deficit Hyperactivity Disorder (ADHD) is identified and assessed. Modern tools, such as digital neuroimaging and sophisticated cognitive assessments, allow for a more precise evaluation of ADHD symptoms. Neuroimaging techniques like fMRI (functional Magnetic Resonance Imaging) provide real-time visuals of brain activity, helping researchers pinpoint areas of dysfunction associated with ADHD. Similarly, computerized attention tests measure various aspects of attention and impulsivity, offering a comprehensive view of the individual's cognitive profile.

Additionally, the development of diagnostic software and artificial intelligence (AI) has enhanced the accuracy and efficiency of ADHD assessments. AI algorithms can analyze vast amounts of data from behavioral assessments and neuroimaging results to identify patterns indicative of ADHD. This not only speeds up the diagnostic process but also improves diagnostic accuracy by reducing human error and bias. These advanced tools facilitate early detection and intervention, which are crucial for the effective management of ADHD.

Moreover, the integration of wearable technology, such as smartwatches that monitor activity levels and behavioral patterns, has introduced a new dimension to ADHD diagnostics.

These devices provide continuous data on a person's activity and attention levels, offering valuable insights that can inform diagnosis and treatment plans. The combination of these advanced tools is paving the way for a more nuanced understanding of ADHD and personalized treatment approaches.

# NEW TREATMENT MODALITIES

The landscape of ADHD treatment has expanded significantly with the introduction of new modalities that go beyond traditional medication. Non-stimulant medications, such as atomoxetine and guanfacine, offer alternative options for individuals who may not respond well to stimulant medications or experience adverse effects. These medications work by targeting different neurotransmitter systems in the brain, providing a tailored approach to managing ADHD symptoms. They are particularly beneficial for individuals who require a non-stimulant approach due to comorbid conditions or sensitivities.

In addition to pharmacological treatments, behavioral therapies have seen significant advancements. Cognitive Behavioral Therapy (CBT) has been adapted to address ADHD-specific challenges, focusing on improving organizational skills, time management, and impulse control. New therapeutic approaches, such as digital CBT programs and app-based interventions, offer accessible and flexible options for managing ADHD symptoms. These digital solutions provide interactive exercises and tools that can be used in real time, making therapy more engaging and practical for daily life.

Moreover, there is a growing emphasis on integrative approaches that combine traditional treatments with lifestyle modifications. Mindfulness-based interventions and physical exercise programs have been shown to enhance attention and reduce hyperactivity. Research supports the benefits of integrating these modalities into a comprehensive treatment plan, offering a holistic approach to managing ADHD. This multifaceted strategy helps address various aspects of ADHD, leading to improved overall functioning and well-being.

## THE ROLE OF GENETICS AND PERSONALIZED MEDICINE

Genetics plays a crucial role in the development and understanding of ADHD, with research uncovering specific genes associated with the disorder. Recent studies have identified several genetic markers linked to ADHD, such as variations in dopamine receptor genes. These findings provide insights into the biological underpinnings of ADHD and help in developing more targeted treatment approaches. Personalized medicine utilizes this genetic information to tailor interventions based on an individual's genetic profile, optimizing treatment effectiveness and reducing the likelihood of adverse reactions.

Personalized medicine also involves the use of pharmacogenomics to predict how individuals will respond to specific medications. By analyzing genetic variations that affect drug metabolism, healthcare providers can select medications that are more likely to be effective and have fewer side effects. This approach ensures that treatments are customized to the individual's genetic makeup, improving the chances of successful management of ADHD symptoms.

Furthermore, the integration of genetic research into clinical practice is enhancing our understanding of ADHD as a multifaceted disorder. By combining genetic data with environmental factors, researchers are gaining a more comprehensive view of ADHD's etiology. This knowledge is driving the development of precision medicine strategies that aim to address the unique needs of each individual, ultimately leading to more effective and personalized treatment options.

## IMPACT OF SOCIETAL CHANGES ON ADHD UNDERSTANDING

Societal changes have significantly influenced the perception and understanding of ADHD, leading to a more nuanced view of the disorder. Increased awareness and advocacy efforts have contributed to greater recognition of ADHD as a legitimate and impactful condition. Public education campaigns and media coverage have helped to dispel myths and reduce stigma, making it easier for individuals and families to seek diagnosis and treatment.

Moreover, shifts in educational and workplace environments have prompted changes in how ADHD is accommodated and managed. Schools and employers are increasingly adopting inclusive practices and providing support systems for individuals with ADHD. This includes implementing individualized education plans (IEPs) and workplace adjustments that address specific needs, such as flexible scheduling and organizational tools. These adaptations help individuals with ADHD thrive in various settings and improve their overall quality of life.

Additionally, the growing focus on mental health and well-being has highlighted the importance of addressing ADHD within the broader context of mental health care. Societal recognition of the interconnectedness of mental health conditions has led to more integrated approaches to treatment and support.

This holistic perspective encourages collaboration between healthcare providers, educators, and employers, fostering a supportive environment that promotes understanding and effective management of ADHD.

# CHAPTER ELEVEN

## COMMON CONCERNS AND DETAILED FAQS

### WHAT IS THE DIFFERENCE BETWEEN ADHD AND ADD?

Attention Deficit Hyperactivity Disorder (ADHD) and Attention Deficit Disorder (ADD) are terms often used interchangeably, but they refer to different conditions.

ADHD is the umbrella term used to describe a spectrum of disorders characterized by symptoms of inattention, hyperactivity, and impulsivity. ADD, specifically, is an outdated term that was used before the current classification system. Now, ADHD is divided into three types: predominantly inattentive presentation, predominantly hyperactive-impulsive presentation, and combined presentation.

The primary difference between these types lies in the symptoms that dominate. The inattentive presentation focuses on difficulties with attention and focus, whereas the hyperactive-impulsive presentation centers on excessive movement and impulsivity. The combined presentation includes significant symptoms from both categories. This distinction helps in tailoring the treatment approaches and understanding the unique challenges faced by individuals with different presentations of ADHD.

Understanding these distinctions is crucial for accurate diagnosis and effective intervention. Proper identification of the symptoms and their type allows for a more targeted approach to managing ADHD, ensuring that both the child and their caregivers can implement strategies suited to their specific needs.

## HOW IS ADHD DIAGNOSED?

Diagnosing ADHD involves a comprehensive evaluation process that includes gathering information from multiple sources. Healthcare providers typically start by conducting a detailed clinical interview with the child and their parents.

This interview covers the child's medical history, developmental milestones, behavioral patterns, and family history of ADHD or related conditions. Observation of the child's behavior in different settings—such as at home and school—also plays a critical role.

In addition to interviews, standardized rating scales and behavioral questionnaires are often used to assess symptoms. These tools help in quantifying the severity of symptoms and their impact on daily functioning. The evaluation may also involve input from teachers or other professionals who interact with the child regularly, providing a well-rounded view of the child's behavior and challenges in various environments.

It is important to rule out other conditions that may present with similar symptoms, such as anxiety or learning disabilities. The diagnosis of ADHD is typically made based on criteria outlined in the Diagnostic and Statistical Manual of Mental Disorders (DSM-5), which requires that symptoms be present for at least six months and cause significant impairment in multiple areas of life.

## WHAT ARE THE COMMON SIDE EFFECTS OF ADHD MEDICATIONS?

Medications used to treat ADHD, such as stimulants and non-stimulants, can have a range of side effects. Common stimulant medications, like methylphenidate and amphetamines, often cause side effects such as decreased appetite, insomnia, and stomachaches.

Some children may also experience increased anxiety or irritability. These side effects are usually dose-dependent and can vary from person to person.

Non-stimulant medications, such as atomoxetine and guanfacine, also have their own set of potential side effects. Atomoxetine may cause drowsiness, decreased appetite, or mood swings, while guanfacine can lead to fatigue or dizziness. Monitoring and adjusting the medication dosage can help mitigate these effects, and working closely with a healthcare provider is essential to finding the right balance.

Understanding and managing these side effects is crucial for ensuring that the medication's benefits outweigh any potential drawbacks. Regular follow-up with a healthcare provider allows for adjustments and support to manage any adverse effects effectively.

## CAN ADHD BE MANAGED WITHOUT MEDICATION?

Managing ADHD without medication involves a combination of behavioral strategies, environmental modifications, and lifestyle changes. Behavioral therapy can help children develop coping skills, improve organizational abilities, and enhance self-control. Techniques such as positive reinforcement, setting clear expectations, and using visual aids can support behavior modification and improve daily functioning.

Environmental adjustments can also be beneficial. Creating a structured routine, reducing distractions, and providing a consistent and supportive environment for children with ADHD to manage their symptoms more effectively. Additionally, lifestyle changes such as regular physical exercise, a balanced diet, and adequate sleep contribute to overall well-being and can help mitigate ADHD symptoms.

While medication is often a key component of ADHD management, non-medication approaches offer valuable alternatives or complementary strategies. Working with healthcare professionals to develop a comprehensive plan tailored to the child's needs can lead to effective management of ADHD symptoms without solely relying on medication.

## HOW CAN PARENTS SUPPORT A CHILD WITH ADHD?

Parents play a crucial role in supporting a child with ADHD by implementing consistent strategies and fostering a supportive environment. Establishing a structured routine with clear expectations and regular schedules helps children with ADHD manage their time and tasks more effectively.

Positive reinforcement, such as praise and rewards for completed tasks, encourages desired behaviors and builds self-esteem.

Creating an organized and distraction-free environment also aids in minimizing challenges associated with ADHD. Tools such as visual schedules, timers, and reminders can help children stay on track and manage their responsibilities. Additionally, involving the child in setting goals and creating strategies for managing their symptoms fosters a sense of ownership and self-efficacy.

Open communication with teachers and healthcare providers is essential for coordinating efforts and addressing any challenges that arise. By staying informed and actively participating in the child's treatment plan, parents can ensure that they are providing the best possible support and creating an environment that fosters growth and success for their child with ADHD.